Slithering S

Boa Constrictors

GAIL TERP

BLACK RABBIT BOOKS

Bolt is published by Black Rabbit Books
P.O. Box 3263, Mankato, Minnesota, 56002.
www.blackrabbitbooks.com

Marysa Storm, editor; Grant Gould, designer;
Omay Ayres, photo researcher

Names: Terp, Gail, 1951- author.
Title: Boa constrictors / by Gail Terp.
Description: Mankato, Minnesota : Black Rabbit Books, [2021] | Series: Bolt. slithering snakes | Includes bibliographical references and index.
Audience: Ages 8-12 | Audience: Grades 4-6 | Summary: "Diagrams, graphs, and fun text help readers explore the habitats, diets, and daily lives of boa constrictors"- Provided by publisher.
Identifiers: LCCN 2019026731 (print) | LCCN 2019026732 (ebook) | ISBN 9781623102715 (hardcover) | ISBN 9781644663677 (paperback) | ISBN 9781623103651 (ebook)
Subjects: LCSH: Boa constrictor–Juvenile literature.
Classification: LCC QL666.O63 T47 2021 (print) | LCC QL666.O63 (ebook) | DDC 597.96/7-dc23
LC record available at https://lccn.loc.gov/2019026731
LC ebook record available at https://lccn.loc.gov/2019026732

Special thanks to Jessica McCarthy for her help with this book.

Printed in the United States. 2/20

Image Credits

Age Fotostock: Geoff Trinder / ardea.com, 21; Alamy: BIOSPHOTO, 17; Joe Blossom, 22–23; Nature Picture Library, 6; AP Images: Jaelyn deMaria, 22; correre.org: Correre, 12 (top left); Dreamstime: Mauro Rodrigues, 12 (btm right); iStock: amattel, 18 (snakes); m.facebook.com: Redland's Snake Catcher, 4–5; Minden Pictures: Eric Baccega, 16; Michael D. Kern, Cover; National Geographic Image Collection: MIKE GUZMAN, 28–29; Newscom: Karl Switak/NHPA/Photoshot, 11 (btm); Science Source: Nature's Images, 12 (top right); Paul Whitten, 26–27; Shutterstock: Aleksandr Sulga, 24 (human); AndreySkat, 24 (lizard); Audrey Snider-Bell, 1; clarst5, 24 (bird); critterbiz, 12 (btm left logs); cynoclub, 24 (young boa); Eric Isselee, 6–7, 14, 20 (adult silhouette); fivespots, 3, 8–9, 31, 32; Independent birds, 24 (bat); Morphart Creation, 14–15; Patrick K. Campbell, 24 (adult boa); PiggingFoto, 12 (btm left snake); Rosa Jay, 20 (newborn silhouette); serkan mutan, 24 (hawk); Simon Laprida, 18 (bkgd); Vaclav Sebek, 24 (caiman); vitormarigo, 11 (top)
Every effort has been made to contact copyright holders for material reproduced in this book. Any omissions will be rectified in subsequent printings if notice is given to the publisher.

CONTENTS

CHAPTER 1

Boa Constrictors in ACTION

It's nighttime. A boa **constrictor** waits on a tree branch. A bat flies toward the tree. It doesn't know the snake is there. Slowly, the boa opens its mouth wide. At the perfect moment, the snake strikes. Its razor-sharp teeth hold the bat. The snake then wraps its powerful body around the animal and squeezes. When the bat is dead, the boa swallows it whole.

WEIGHT

60 TO 100 POUNDS
(27 to 45 kilograms)

Blending In

Boa constrictors are large snakes. Their bodies are often tan or brown with colored bands and spots. Marked this way, the snakes blend in with their surroundings. **Prey** has trouble seeing them.

How Big Is a Boa Constrictor?

BOA CONSTRICTOR FEATURES

POWERFUL MUSCLES
SMOOTH SKIN

CHAPTER 2

HUNTING and Homes

Boa constrictors are **ambush** hunters. They wait for prey to come close. Then they attack. The snakes then kill by squeezing.

Boas eat bats and squirrels. They also eat lizards and birds. If an animal fits in their mouths, the snakes will eat it.

Scientists thought constrictors killed prey by keeping animals from breathing. Now they believe the snakes kill by stopping blood flow. Without blood, the animals' hearts stop.

RAIN FORESTS

WOODS

HOLLOW LOGS

GRASSLANDS

Different Homes

Boa constrictors are found in Central and South America. They live in many different places. Some boas live on the edges of rain forests. Others live in woods and grasslands. Many boas hang out in trees or near streams. Others live in **hollow** logs or abandoned **burrows**.

Some boas hang in cave entrances. The snakes catch bats as they fly out.

WHERE BOA CONSTRICTORS LIVE

Boa Constrictor Range Map

Boa Constrictors in Florida

Boa constrictors don't normally live in the United States. But people have brought some to the area as pets. Some now live in the wild in Florida.

Pet owners released the snakes after they got too big. Other snakes escaped. These snakes are causing problems. They **prey** on small animals in the area. Some of those animals are **endangered**.

Boa constrictors are good swimmers. They don't often go in water, though.

CHAPTER 3

FAMILY Life

Boa constrictors usually live alone. But males and females come together to **mate** during spring and summer. Females don't mate every year. When they're ready, they give out a scent. Males follow the scent to find them.

Baby Snakes

Unlike some other snakes, boas give birth to live babies. The young are **independent** right after they're born. Their mothers don't take care of them.

Young boas start life knowing how to hunt. They often hunt in trees. When they grow heavier, they hunt more on the ground.

COMPARING SIZES

BY THE NUMBERS

about
3 years old
AGE WHEN BOA CONSTRICTORS CAN HAVE BABIES

25
AVERAGE NUMBER OF BABIES MOTHERS HAVE AT ONE TIME

18 FEET
(5 m)
LONGEST BOA CONSTRICTOR RECORDED

20 to 30 years
LIFE SPAN

Boa Constrictor Food Chain

This food chain shows what eats boa constrictors. It also shows what boa constrictors eat.

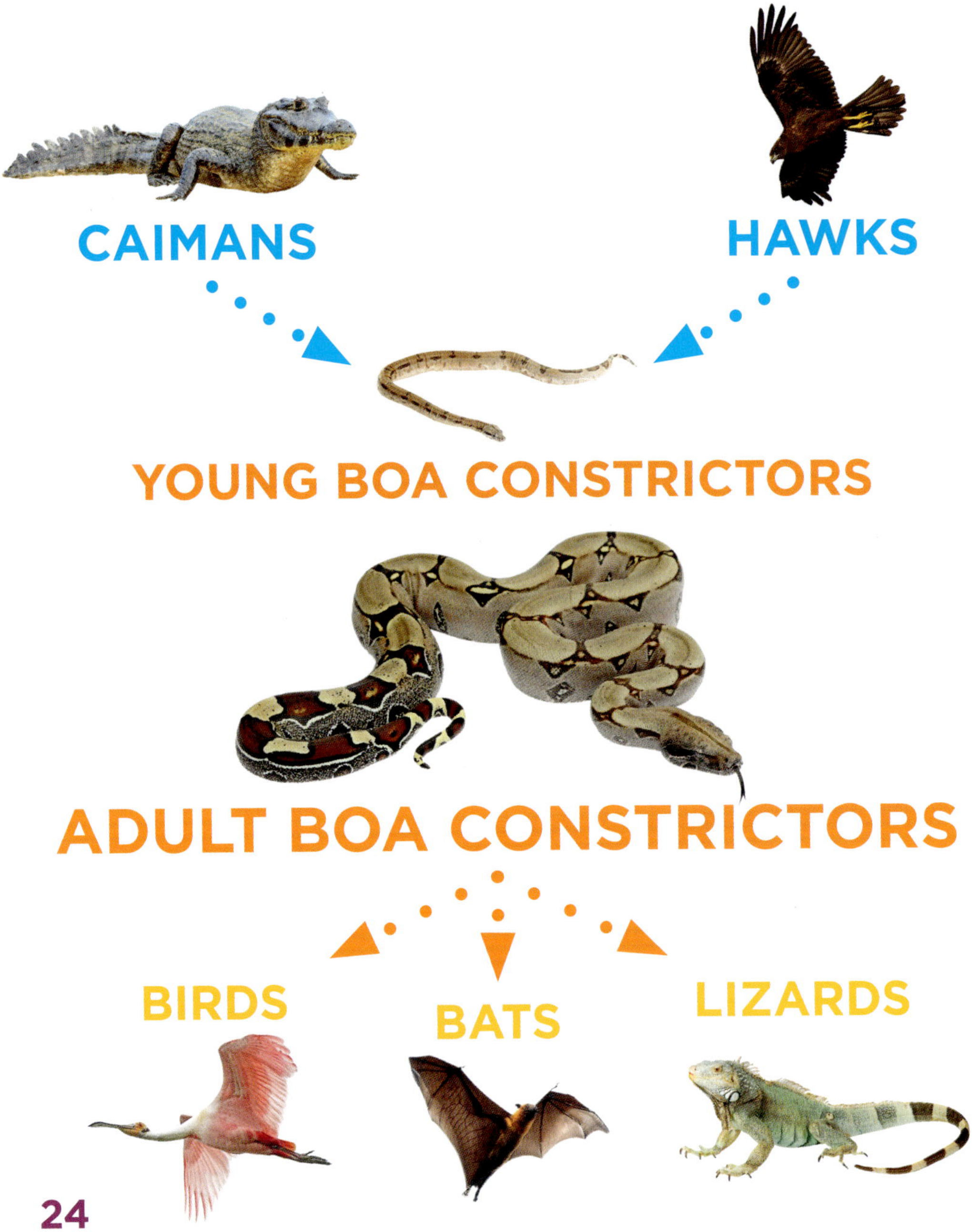

CHAPTER 4

Part of THEIR WORLD

Adult boas are at the top of the food chain. But some animals, such as hawks and **caimans**, eat young ones. Humans are an even bigger threat.

People hunt boa constrictors for their meat. They kill boas for their skins too. They even trap the snakes to sell as pets. Humans also build where boas live. The snakes have less land to live on.

A Help to Humans

Boa constrictors often help humans. They kill pests, such as rats. They also kill opossums. Opossums can spread a deadly disease. By eating opossums, boas help control the disease. They keep the disease from passing to humans.

Slithering On

Boa constrictors play a key part in the food chain. The young provide food to some animals. Adults help control other animal populations. Boa constrictors are not in danger of disappearing right now. But if humans keep destroying their habitats, the snakes could be in danger. It's up to humans to keep these amazing snakes safe.

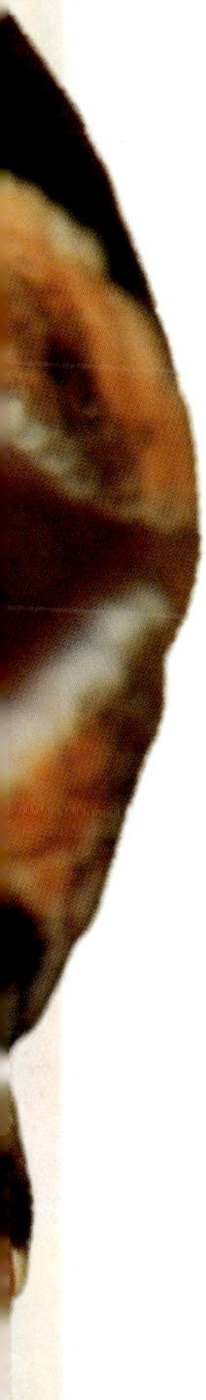

Boa teeth often fall out. The snakes just grow new teeth.

ambush (AM-buhsh)—to attack by surprise

burrow (BUR-oh)—a hole in the ground made by an animal for shelter or protection

caiman (KAY-muhn)—a type of reptile in the crocodile family

constrictor (kuhn-STRIK-tur)—a snake that coils around and squeezes prey

endangered (in-DAYN-jurd)—close to becoming extinct

hollow (HAWL-oh)—an unfilled space

independent (in-di-PEN-duhnt)—not relying on anyone or anything else

mate (MAYT)—to join together to produce young

prey (PRAY)—an animal hunted or killed for food; it also means to catch and eat something.

LEARN MORE

BOOKS

Bankston, John. *Boa Constrictors*. All about Snakes. Hallandale, FL: Mitchell Lane Publishers, 2019.

Kenan, Tessa. *It's a Boa Constrictor!* Rain Forest Animals. Minneapolis: Lerner Publications, 2017.

Kenney, Karen Latchana. *Life Cycle of a Snake*. Incredible Animal Life Cycles. Minneapolis: Pogo, 2019.

WEBSITES

Boa Constrictor
kids.nationalgeographic.com/animals/boa-constrictor/#boa-constrictor-closeup.jpg

Boa Constrictor Facts for Kids
sciencing.com/boa-constrictor-kids-5776740.html

Boa Constrictors Facts for Kids
easyscienceforkids.com/all-about-boa-constrictors/

INDEX